UNDER THE
PALM TREE

A Journey from Childhood to Retirement

PAULIE THE BALLIE

Copyright © 2019 by Paulie the Ballie.

ISBN   Softcover   978-1-949723-86-1
                 eBook   978-1-950580-50-7

All rights reserved. No part of this book may be reproduced or transmitted in any form or by any means, electronic or mechanical, including photocopying, recording, or by any information storage and retrieval system without express written permission from the author, except in the case of brief quotations embodied in critical reviews and certain other non-commercial uses permitted by copyright law.

Printed in the United States of America.

To order additional copies of this book, contact:
Bookwhip
1-855-339-3589
https://www.bookwhip.com

CONTENTS

Foreword 1
The Formative Years 2
The Young Man 9
The Paris Connection 11
Epilogue 20
Epilogue II 22
The Operation 36
The Stray 39
The Battle of Chancellorsville 42
A Tale of Two Pins 45
The Choice 48
The Torch 50
The Trip 51
The Collaborators 53
The Encounter 55
The Game 57
The Feeling 58
The Balladeer 60
Epilogue!!! 61
Aftermath Lament 62
This Election 63
Thank You 64
1907 66
Epilogue IV 68
The Winsome Spring 70
A Farewell 71
The Briar Patch 72

Breath 73
The Walmart Girl 74
Prologue & An Open Letter to My Young Readers 75
Letter to Tampa Bay Times 77
Two Chicks at My Door 79
O Walt 80
Define Destiny 81
The Child of Mosul 82
In Closing 83
After Thought 84

My humble effort is inspired completely by the heroic actions of the many first responders and medical staff that come into the fray without questions to save lives and, most of all, our brave law enforcement officers, who disregard their own safety to protect us. I hope each one of those kind souls have a guardian angel to keep them safe and well so each one of them can also, one day, get *Under the Palm Tree*.

FOREWORD

The latest statistics on the population of the Sunshine State is just shy of twenty million. Most came here from all points of the compass, mainly from the cooler parts of our nation, seeking a warmer climate and access to the best fishing, golfing, boating and other outdoor activities. All the aforementioned were duly delivered, but what we did not expect was the mismanagement of our elected officials to cause financial problems with little relief on the horizon.

Bad weather, a greedy insurance industry that deserted the state and left it to incompetent politicians to keep the cost of property insurance affordable, was a complete failure and threatened to put an end to those great dreams for many Floridians who lived on fixed incomes.

Also, the failure to recognize that global warming is adversely affecting our climate, causing terrible storms wreaking havoc from coast to coast, is another dilemma.

The recent reelection of Barack Obama and his carrying the usually red state of Florida were hopeful signs that, maybe, we will start dealing with various threats to the general welfare of all our citizens and that we can restore that dream for one and all.

The following is a fictional account of one person's journey from childhood to retirement in Florida. Maybe the reader will see a little of themselves in this account. If not, maybe a few chuckles.

I stand, still hopeful, that in spite of all the problems that face us today, we will, with the newly elected president, deal effectually with restoring that dream, "another day in paradise."

THE FORMATIVE YEARS

"Well, now here's the deal, Bubba. You tell the story, or I am going to bust you up."

"Now wait a minute. Who do you think you are?"

"Yeah, I am just a figgie of your mind, but I can creep into your head and keep you up at night, and furthermore, I can screw up your golf game by bringing up some bad thoughts while putting."

"Okay, okay, you win."

"Where do we start?"

"How about One Benedict Place?"

"The year is 1939. The place—the largest unincorporated village in Northern United States. Pure suburbia and plenty of still-undeveloped land stretching from Grand Avenue to Milburn Avenue. Mostly inhabited by executives working in the Big Apple. Your pop is one, working for IBM at their Madison Avenue offices. He is in their Public Relations Department and Advertising Section. Now take it from there, Bubba."

Being a small lad with lots of enthusiasm, I am reminded of the great summers with the crickets singing their songs. I can still smell those burning leaves as though it were yesterday. I remember that empty lot in the back of the houses where we made a small ball field, playing there every summer night until dark when time stood still. Having a buddy to talk to and share the wonders around us with was paramount.

Every night before sleeping, leaning out of my window facing the house adjacent to the right, I conversed with another lad, young Jimmy Quinn, sharing what happened that day and what we might do the following day. We became great pals, and every night, we formed a very strong bond. Suddenly, Jimmy was not there. After several days, I went over to the house to see why. Jimmy's older brother said, "Sorry to tell you that Jimmy passed away after fighting diabetes." I nodded to show that I understood, but inside, I didn't, and *why* became a very large issue for me.

The comradery at this age is, without a doubt, the strongest and most vital and sets the tone for future relationships. Although I missed our conversations, I had, and until this day, a feeling that Jimmy was with me, maybe to share things he was denied at such a young age. Perhaps he became my guardian angel, who had to work overtime on several occasions.

As the quiet of homelife slowly eroded away with arguments, divorce in the cards, and Pop drinking too much and losing his job, the next thing I knew, Pop was packing up and leaving that day by cab. Mom was upset, and things got tough: with less money, we had to sell our pride and joy, a 1941 Mercury.

The next thing I knew was, a new guy was moving into the house, an army officer whom we will call the Rat. Similar last name. Now this dude was also a drinker and, when drinking, became mean. One night, I was in my bed, sitting up, and the Rat came in and yelled something and slammed my head back into the wall behind. Well, now this was a lesson to me that sometimes, things went wrong, and one must be prepared and on guard. So, I made a plan. If the Rat tried this again, then I will run out the back door and run around the house, knowing that he will follow. There was a four-foot fence on the left side of the house, which I had learned to jump over without any problem.

Sure enough, drinking again, he charged up into my room on the second floor, and I slipped by him and ran out the back door. Hearing him in pursuit, I ran like a deer, flying over the fence, and two minutes later, I heard a loud groan, and sure enough, the Rat ran into it, got really banged up, and had to get medical attention. Funny, he never bothered with me again.

Now the plan was to send me out to Kansas to spend the summer with my father, who was now living with his mother and her second husband, a Southern Baptist minister. So, the Rat took me to the train station, and I remember him saying, "I really love your mom and will take good care of her." I got on the train with a sense of anticipation, going out West where there were cowboys and horses. I had just seen the movie *Red River* with John Wayne, and boy, did I look forward to that trip.

By the by, I never saw the Rat again. On the train, I had a compartment, two bunks, upper and lower. The trip took two nights, and I slept on the lower the first night and upper the last night. The welcome was truly great. Both Grandma and the preacher picked me up.

Grandma was a French and Cherokee Indian and had married my real grandfather, who was English and German. When I was four years of age, he visited us and brought me a real Indian headdress. He was a wiry man with blond hair. Unfortunately, that marriage did not last as well. His papa fought in the Civil War and was reported to have been at Gettysburg.

Grandma took me home with them, and I spent the next eight years out West. The following is that experience: I settled in quite well. Now the church in a small town like this (population 6,400) was the center of social life. Prayer meetings on Wednesdays and two services on Sundays, several picnics, and community dinners were the norm.

After each sermon, there was always an invitation to give oneself to Christ, and sure enough, I made the walk up the aisle to a chorus of praise to the Lord. That next Sunday, I was baptized in a tank of water that was directly behind the altar. A strong feeling of calmness cascaded like a fountain of tears throughout my body, a very unique experience, which remains with me till today.

A young girl, about sixteen years of age, became my first real friend out there. We went together to church and carnivals and became very close that first year. One day, I went to her house and heard her telling someone, whom I later found out was her father, "Oh, not again, please don't." After that, I never really saw her again as she moved away suddenly.

Now football was really big out there, and the games were attended by the entire town. Playing that game was pretty tough for a very skinny kid, and I was the skinniest kid in town. One could see my ribs sticking out, and many a time, people marveled at how skinny a kid I was.

Now the old man was still drinking but managing to earn a living with a small advertising agency. Pop did his own artwork and was very adept with ads for newspapers and periodicals. He started a new office in Tulsa, Oklahoma, and we moved there, renting a room in a fine house in a good neighborhood. He took up with a lady who ran a beauty shop, and the next thing I knew, we were living in her one-bedroom apartment. I was sleeping on the couch in the living room as I had at Grandma's in Kansas.

One day, after school, I was sitting in the living room and had my feet on the table, and she threw a fit, telling Pop that I had to go. So, Pop took me to find a furnished room in the two-story wooden-frame dwelling that had a small screened porch in the rear. The room was small but ample, and I felt good about having my own place to live in.

The next day, school started, and I got up and walked to school, which was not too far away. The first day, as I walked up the entrance, a tall lanky dark-haired guy was standing on the top step and appeared to be looking for someone and said, "Hey, my name is Bob." The school was quite cliquish, and little groups were quickly formed, and come hell or high water, if one was not a part of those groups, then they remained an outsider and totally ignored.

So, finding Bob was great, and we met after school each day, going to the local pool hall, which had all the wire services keeping track of all sports activity, baseball scores, etc. The smoke in the room was heavy enough to be cut with a knife, but no one seemed to mind. Snooker was the game of choice, and lots of money changed hands. One member of Tulsa's basketball team was a regular player, and he had an eye just like his jump shot, which was on the mark more times than not.

Now Bob left suddenly too, telling me one day that his family was moving, and I said in response, "What will I do?" Bob replied, "You'll find someone," and that I did. I met up with Irv after joining the Red Shield Club in Tulsa. We became involved in basketball and tennis. We played for a local church team and got together after school and spent the entire summer as great pals. But Irv, who was a member of the National Guard, got called up for duty in Korea, and the next thing I knew, he was shipping out. So, I got together a little going-away deal for him, borrowing a car and collecting some cash so he could go on a big date with his lovely girlfriend. So off he went, and I never heard from him after that. It seemed that those you get buddies with go their way without much fanfare. Saying good-bye was just par for the course.

Every weekend, a bus picked us up at the Red Shield Club to transport us to Southern Hills, a private country club, to caddy for the rich oil tycoons who were members there. The pro there was a very nice guy by the name of Bill Witherspoon, who took a very keen interest in helping caddies out. Mr. W. became the treasurer of the PGA. Mr. W. was a great putter and very straight off the tee.

One day, a group of us caddies, who played thirty-six holes on caddy day, decided to go to a St. Louis and Dodger's ball game to see the likes of Stan Musial, Duke Snider, and Jackie Robinson. This encompassed a 350-mile drive in a 1936 Chevy with a sleepover in the public park nearby the ballpark. So, we all took sleeping bags, and off we went. To say the least, it was not a peaceful night as a very strange guy tried to grab one of us, and I heard our driver say, "Hey, you better hit the road, you jawboney, or I am going to knock your block off." He took off, but it was very difficult to sleep after that. Needless to say, this Bubba couldn't keep his eyes open during the game and missed most of it. We got back home safe and sound.

I seldom saw my father since I moved out, but it was just as well as the wicked witch of the north was not missed at all. One day, while sitting in the barbershop to get a haircut, the barber looked at me and said, "I can hear that boy's hair growing from here." The drugstore was next door, and one day, while in there on an errand, the lady behind the counter called me over and said, "I hear, you are graduating from high school, and I would like you to have this." I looked at the ten dollars in her hand and said, "Thank you very much." I didn't even know her name.

Now living in this room had some really strange moments. One night, I noticed a bright light go on just next door, and behold, the shade was up, and a girl, naked as a jaybird, was standing in front of a mirror. She was beautiful with very dark hair, and I, at once, recognized her as the girl I spoke to in the local café where I was eating breakfast most mornings before school.

This happened almost every night, and finally, one night, I said, "Psst, can I come over?" The reply was, "Who is it?" I replied, "Your friend from the café." The light went off, and I sat in my room with the light out. I saw her and a guy looking around the yard. Playing very cool, I said not a word, being very surprised to see a guy with her as I never saw anyone else in the room.

Later that week, I saw her in the café again, and she came up to me and said, "My friend is away for a few days." Then I heard you again whisper in my ear, "Leave it alone, Bubba. She's taken. Don't get involved. Your time will come." I never saw her again. But gosh, she was a real beauty.

Before I left that room for the Big Apple after the summer following high school graduation, I was walking home from a day of caddying at Southern Hills, a private country club that held the US Open twice and the PGA twice. A gang of guys saw me, and they yelled, "Hey you, come here." Well, then you shouted in my ear, "Run, get out of here," and run I did, streaking toward that screened porch at the rear of my boarding house, slipping in, panting quickly, latching the screened door, and lying prone on the floor, heart beating ferociously, hearing voices saying, "Where the hell is he?" and "Boy, he was fast." I am happy to say I never found out what they wanted from me.

Thinking back on this, I have found out that survival is not a thing of chance but a desire to live, shared by all, and that first instance of danger is an alarm that gives the impetus to take action to avoid the impending threat.

THE YOUNG MAN

Okay, Bubba, you had graduated from high school. The plan was to return to the Big Apple to your mom, look for a college, and find some direction for your life. So, Pop took you to the Greyhound Station for the ride to your new home.

The parting was very formal without any emotion as Pop seemed to be relieved of the responsibility. Mom was now married to her third husband, a PR man who had his own business. He was involved in the national politics and was working on the "I like Ike" campaign.

They got you a summer job at a fishing resort on the very end of Long Island. This resort had a very large pier, which served as a submarine base during the WWII. There were approximately thirty boats docked there.

During the summer, there was a train leaving Penn Station very early so that it arrived at the end of line, Montauk Point Station, around 8:00 am, which was located adjacent to the pier. As soon as the train arrived, hundreds of fishermen jumped off and ran toward the boats, tackled boxes, and flapped in the air for the dash to get on their favorite boat as soon as possible. It was really something to see.

You worked in the bait and tackle shop and learned how to gut and clean the catch. Although you smelled very fishy, you didn't mind as the tips were good. One of the workers sold you the first car you ever owned, a Model A Roadster with a canvas top and a rumble seat. You paid $50 for it, but here's the catch: you couldn't afford the insurance, so you drove for several weeks without a license. This was possible because there was only one policeman on duty, and you knew his routine and drove the car when he was out of the area.

What a car. Great power in third gear and real fun driving on the sand dunes. You eventually sold the car to your boss, a Norwegian who wanted it for a beach buggy. You got $45 for it. Not bad for having had wheels all summer.

Occasionally, you went into the next town, East Hampton, to roller-skate. You met a young girl and became interested in each other. After one night of very intense necking, her mom spoke to you the next day, saying her daughter was not ready for this very intense kissing, etc., and bingo, that ended that. I told you not to worry, being eighteen years old with plenty of time to find someone.

One day, after the boats came in, one of the captains stopped by and started talking about himself. He was a tall, handsome sort, Irish to the core, and served with JFK in the South Pacific during WWII and never got a scratch. He was a graduate of Columbia Journalism School, which he got under the GI Bill. He also did some acting in movies. He told me that after the summer, he planned to marry. His boat, the *Pelican*, was the most popular of all. Everyone tried to get on it. Usually, there were some eighty people on board, which included the captain and one first mate.

Toward the end of the season, right before Labor Day, a very windy, rainy front suddenly came in shortly after the boats left the dock. Disaster struck. I heard my boss running down the pier, yelling, "The *Pelican* is down, the *Pelican* is down." Sadly, only nineteen survived, and sixty-nine people drowned. They never found the captain. He went down with his boat. The first mate, who had borrowed a pair of my blue jeans, made it back and survived. The sadness and despair were an immensely terrible ending to the summer, leaving us with a huge sense of loss.

I then entered college and, after one year, dropped out and got drafted the day the Korean War ended. Thanks to Ike, who, history tells us, ended that war as he had promised during his campaign. Thanks to Ike, I did not have to worry about being shot on that frozen peninsula and am able to write about it on this day. I not only liked Ike, but I also loved him. I hope he has a tee time in the hereafter.

THE PARIS CONNECTION

Your basic training was done in Indiana with some maneuvers in Wisconsin and went pretty well until you drew guard duty during the wee hours of the night. Your duty encompassed standing out on the artillery range with a small club. No weapon was permitted.

Now this range was located in the outer regions of Camp McCoy near Madison, Wisconsin, very cold with a very active bear population. Now you asked yourself, *Who, in the hell, thought this one up? What good is a small club to do against a big black bear who may be looking for a tasty snack, namely moi?*

So, you took a chance, telling the corporal of the guard to drop you off at the motor pool to take a Jeep to use for warmth. Letting the engine run with a small cardboard in front of the motor gave a real warm temp inside the vehicle. It was simply great.

When you were relieved, the next guy on guard duty begged on his knees for you to leave the Jeep with him. You told him that that Jeep must be returned to the motor pool before the colonel arrived on the range that next morning. So, what happened? The Jeep was not returned and was standing on the range for all to see.

The next thing you knew, the first sarge was running through the barracks, screaming, "You SOBs, we are going to find out who did this, and that person is looking at stockade time and a DD." Well, I had to step up to the plate again, Bubba, and kept everyone quiet. No one said a word. Phew, that was close.

Now you got the marching orders, and most of the company was going to Europe to the German/Russian border. However, when we were being processed at Camp Kilmer in New Jersey, a clerk there suggested that you take a typing test in Germany, and if you passed it, then you could go somewhere else. Sure enough, that typing course you took in high school paid off. Learning the keyboard was the best thing you did. You passed the test, and when you got the orders from EUCOM Headquarters in Paris, France, you screamed and jumped with joy. You even took time to thank me, Bubba. The first thing you noticed was that right across the street was a beautiful golf course, where you played every Monday when not required for duty.

You went into Paris the first night with a fellow serviceman, a marine sergeant. He wanted to go to a bar where there were lady hostesses. You told him, "Under no conditions let them talk you into buying them a drink." I got $30 to spend, and I didn't have any idea how much the sergeant had. Oops, there he went, a bottle of bubbly was on the bar in front of two ladies. Well, when the bar bill came, it was $138 bucks. So, we went down to the restroom to discuss our options. We rejected running for it as there were some tough-looking guys there.

So, the sarge decided to go to the Paris Embassy and get some moola from the marine staff there, and you had to remain hostage until he came back, which took about two hours. Now that seemed like a lifetime. When Sarge returned, we paid the bill and took off. That was the last time Sarge and you went to town as per my suggestion.

Now something remarkable happened to you while sitting in a bar in Pigalle; you got a chance to appear in a French movie with actor Jean Gabin. It was a comedy; you got 1,500 francs for it. Funny, you never got to see it, but a buddy saw it, and you looked good.

Paris was a beautiful city with a super nightlife with night clubs galore and plenty of places to visit. The air had a certain smell unlike anywhere else in the world; maybe it was the many open-air toilets that lined all the streets. Or maybe it was the great bread that the French consumed like water.

UNDER THE PALM TREE

After a while, you got a seven-day pass. You went to the train station and saw about a rail trip to Spain. The clerk there talked about the trip to

Madrid then on to Barcelona and then an overnight boat trip to Palma de Mallorca. It sounded great, and next thing, you're on the train, riding second class with your suitcase above the seat in a rack. There were four other people in the compartment.

You're sleeping very comfortably when a sudden loud noise occurred, and you got whacked when your case fell off the rack and slammed into your noggin. The train had collided with another train, and the next thing, you're off the train, riding a bus several miles to Madrid. Now the bus left everyone at the outskirts of town, and you had to walk three miles to the hotel. A boy offered to carry your suitcase, and off you went. Not to worry, Bubba, I got your back covered.

You slept like a baby, and the next day, you did the usual sightseeing. After two days there, you're off to Barcelona, and you were really impressed with the city with very large roads and plenty of flowers, trees, and shrubs. You checked in that night on the boat for Palma and shared a compartment with three other people.

The next morning, you woke up and found yourself in the harbor, and off you went. After checking in to a bed-and-breakfast and stopping for a drink, the fellow next to you spoke English and stated that "There are seven thousand homosexuals on the island." You thought to yourself, *Does he personally know each one of them?* Anyhow, you left and went on a walk, looking at the beautiful island.

That night, you went nightclubbing until the wee hours of the morning and danced your silly feet off, having a smashing time. The next day, you had a drink in a bar near the harbor. The place was owned by a German, who said he got a lot of Europeans here as this part of the island was a favorite spot. Now what happened next? You behaved very well, Bubba, and I have to congratulate you.

PAULIE THE BALLIE

A beautiful girl entered the bar alone and sat down right next to you. There were two guys sitting at the end of the bar, and they seemed very interested with her and told the bartender to give her whatever she wanted. The owner then told you, "Watch this girl, who is a dancer and will have champagne cocktails and, after a few, will remove her blouse and will sit there topless and may get on the bar and do a dance." Sure enough, right on cue, she calmly removed her blouse. Now the two fellows really got interested and tried their best to pick her up, but much to their dismay, she passed out on the floor, and a cab was called, taking her home.

Wow, this trip was a real gas. Well, the train ride home went without an incident, and back to Paris you went.

You got the traveling bug, and three of you decided to catch the weekly mail flight to Rome. So, the three of you jumped on board with your four-day pass, and off you went. Now the mail flight had bucket seats, and your flight went just fine. One of your fellow travelers was a professional jazz pianist whose family suggested he enlist in the army so he could think about his relationship with a black girl.

We went into a café, and sure enough, it had a piano. So, my buddy started to play the best jazz you ever wanted to hear but not so for the manager, who came running over, telling him to stop. What a jerk. Anyhow, we got out of there, and he decided to rent a motor scooter.

Now although Rome is one of the most beautiful cities in the world, the traffic is horrendous. Rome has several water fountains, and one has to be very cautious when driving around them.

You told me, "Don't get on the scooter with him," which was the best advice as he crashed when getting too close to one of the fountains. The poor boy ended up in the hospital, and we gave him some of our money to help him get home.

So, we continued to Naples, which had some very interesting locations and plenty of side trips, like Capri and Sorrento. What a beautiful country with so much to see. What impressed you the most was the culture, siestas each working day for three hours. Plenty of time to relax and time to reflect on your day and what you had planned for the evening.

You noticed that food and drink were taken very seriously, and the emphasis was to take your time when eating. A true Italian meal includes several courses, and one has to eat a little of each to fully enjoy the meal. The typical family stresses the importance of eating together, and the communication during the meal is friendly and supportive with plenty of respect for all present. You call it the spirit of the meal, which is handed down from generation to generation. The zest of living is relished and savored. No eating on the run here.

All in all, you learned a valuable lesson on the art of living. Enjoying the beauty around us and taking time to taste it are paramount. You held it close and swore to yourself not to forget and to avoid senseless, routine living as life is a gift to be cherished with those you love every day of your journey. We wrapped up the trip and returned to Paris, feeling totally better for it.

Now you told me you had a feeling that someone important would be entering your life soon. Sure enough, it did. Your first real love affair was about to happen.

It happened without warning and out of the blue. You met on the bus to Paris. She worked in the PX. You became lovers for one month before discharge. The intensity of first love is the strongest thing on earth. You were walking on clouds, and what you remember are the small things, like when waiting to meet under the Arc of Triumph, you were feeding the pigeons, and you saw her pink sneakers approaching, and you looked up with a complete feeling that all was well with the world. You both went hand in hand with a sense of well-being. She would go on to say, "You'll never forget me." Not ready for this commitment, we parted after one month, knowing that I would hold this memory close to my heart forever.

Fast forward to present time and to present day. The place—a small golfing community on the West Coast. Only twenty-five miles north of Tampa. Best known for the most reasonable golf fees in the good ole United States of America. Over seventy courses to choose from, including a couple in the top fifty of the best in the country. You are running two tournaments each week with about fifty players in all. You have been doing it for the last ten years. Having fun doing what you started as a lad, ten years of age. Goofing, as you call it, has kept you on an even keel and is the best therapy you could ever ask for.

You run a special hole-in-one tournament each week with a very sizable cash reward. Sometimes, during the past years, a good buddy got one for $4,800. You, as well, got one, which was the thrill of your life, taking a prize of $1,800. Over the course of the past ten years, you have awarded $10,800 in cash prizes to over ten lucky goofers. You try to give back to the community by running local food programs and an occasional tournament for our wounded warriors and their survivors.

You find that your goofers are a very generous group with their support. However, at times, some problems arise with some disgruntled goofers, who teach you that some bring their problems to the course and what is important is recognized for what it is—just a little bleep along the way.

After one tournament, several Snickers bars are missing. From time to time, you give out treats to the golfers as Snickers always go over with a bang. Now where did they go? You are looking for a bag of forty minibars not yet opened. You look everywhere. Wait, one place you didn't look in was the computer room. Sure enough, your briefcase is on the floor, and the Snickers bag is in shreds. You notice that every one of the bars is gone, wrappers and all. Your beagle, Hoppy, has been at it again. You call him over, and he looks at you with the darnest woeful look. You try to scold him, but you can't. If he survives this, then it will be a miracle. Happy to say, his tail continues its rapid movement without skipping a beat. He is just fine. Maybe you should send this to the Mars company as a point of interest.

Right on, Bubba, you got that right. Now you know that deep down, playing golf with your friends and competing with them are the spices of life. Never has a game done so much for retirees. It keeps you young at heart and keeps that social life that is so important for physical and mental health.

One day, however, was not without problems. One of the players got very upset with whom I had paired him with and started a fuss. Some words were exchanged, and he, a large man who had played guard for a major college, said to me, "Take a swing at me." Well, you whispered in my ear again and said, "Wow, here we go again, just tell him you are seventy years of age and no way are you going to take a swing at him." Done deal, no further problem.

Later that year, the same person was playing with the group again, and he hit a ball in a conservation area, which had signs stating, "Do not enter this area with cart as hunting for golf balls is prohibited." Not so for this determined golfer who, to find his ball, drove his cart into the swamp and got stuck; while sinking into the muck and mire, he screamed for help, but his playing partner had already left, taking his clubs off the cart and walking briskly away toward the clubhouse, yelling, "I can't take any more."

Luckily, a ranger came by and called for help to pull the cart to firm ground.

What I learned from this experience was not to sweat the small stuff and, whenever setting pairings for golf, to always have a disclaimer that these pairings are only done as a convenience and it is up to you to say with whom you wished to golf. Good advice as this has worked very well for the last ten years.

You think back to how you were introduced to the game. A friend of your dad, a columnist for a New York paper, set up some holes in your backyard, telling you to just try and get that ball into those holes he had dug. I asked him, "Is that all that it is?" and he replied, "Yes, my young man, that's it." In the years to come, I thank you, Mr. Earl, for taking time with moi. After seventy years of playing this game, I know it has been worth every second.

I hope part of this journey proves entertaining for the reader as it is not just the trip that is meaningful but also the people you love and the love and support you received from many unexpected kind souls along the way.

Some suggestions for a survival kit for retirees in *Under the Palm Tree* are the following:

1. Hug your companion at least once a day, and don't be sparse with *I love you.*
2. Give yourself credit, but don't exceed your limit.
3. Take a safe driver's course to help you deal with the very aggressive drivers now on the road.
4. Learn a hobby, or take up golf, the greatest game known to man.
5. Get a satellite radio and listen to the music of your choice.
6. Give what you can afford to local charities, including our wounded warriors and servicemen and women who are still in harm's way.
7. Have an active social life with friends and family.
8. Take care of your health.
9. Get a pet who will be the best companion you'll ever have. The pound is full of deserving pets that need a loving home.

10. Support politicians that have rational agenda for keeping your benefits alive and well. You worked hard for all those years to get them, and they need to be preserved.
11. Love your country, for it is based on great ideals that all people are created equal and have the right for the pursuit of happiness. One thing is for sure: we, as a nation, become stronger and more resilient when those who wish us harm attack us. These cowardly acts of terror bring us together, binding us to one another as one nation united facing the unknown without fear or trepidation. The message is loud and clear: our country's principles stay firmly in place and will endure as proven so often during these testing times.

"Hey, Bubba, wait a minute, aren't you going to let me say something?"

"Sure, what is it?"

"Happiness and love go hand in hand. Sometimes, love is difficult to recognize as it creeps up on you without warning and gains intensity as it grows. So, grab it and hold it close and realize it's a blessing."

"Okay, what's next?"

"Well, Bubba, I can move on now that you told part of the story."

"Where are you going?"

"Well, maybe Beantown."

"I'll miss you."

"You'll be fine, Bubba. What are you gonna do?"

"Guess I'll stay under the palm tree a while longer."

EPILOGUE

Ship Adrift in Our Year of Our Lord 2008

    What lurks in so many places
    One must be O so selective
    Not without plan or direction
    Less humanity be the poorer
    As war drums beat on with no pause
    Into a fountain of despair
    This day before the '08 election
    Hoping for a champion to steer for the shore
    None too soon say many voices for sure
    May hope for peace be restored
    With a timely end to this war

Roberts Ridge

A day of bullets, a day of blood, a day of courage, a day on the ground, men stood fast, duty bound. Reaching out hands for the fallen. Comrades all young and pure. Crying for instant response. Dismally to no avail. Several hours late, rescue came, too late, too late for the silent eight, who rode home without a word. Oh, what could have been just a few hours less at best.

A Dedication to the American Voter 2008 and 2012

Seldom has the torch of freedom burned so brightly
Our hopes have once again risen to new heights
Off years of stumbling we all knew
That like crisis before, the nation would prevail
Now together, strong and resolute, a determined people

Casting away those idolaters of hate and fear at last so clear
Of course, there will be some doubters; there always are. Let them rant to no avail Those lackeys of despair. Be gone, we say, be gone, no use here For all the world to see there's a new day, a new way. Barack Obama, the president of the USA

EPILOGUE II

Hey Bubba, "Our story isn't quite right you know". ": What do you mean"? Well for starters you left out 1943 and that the trip in 1939 to LaGuardia to see off Ms. Beebe Daniels & her Hubby Ben Lyons. Right you are. Okay Bubba let's give it a go.

The year early 1939, London is under attack. It's very dangerous to be there now. But not so for Ms. Daniels and her Husband Ben Lyons. They are departing today on PAN Clipper to return to their Country to offer their support. They will eventually have a radio program offering solace during those horrific years. Giving up lucrative careers and the safety of Hollywood was never in question. Truly a prime example of that entire Country who came together as one. They continued to be a determined people fulfilling their legacy set so long ago when Queen Elizabeth rallied the country to resist the Spanish Armada. The rest of of course is history.

Well your Pop took you with him on that day and you met Ms. Daniels and Mr. Lyons. Pop took you on the Clipper. Their drawing room was spacious and comfortable for that long flight. Ms. Daniels was very gracious to this 6-year-old and I still remember her kind words. I thought I noticed a determined, positive state of mind with both Ms. Daniels and Mr. Lyons. A hearty goodbye was expressed by all present. As the clipper skipped along the waterway for takeoff a rainbow was seen, and all present thought well of it. A very good omen to say the least.

In early 1943, the family still together moved to Washington, D.C when your Pop took a leave of absence from I.B.M. and went to set up and promote the "Thumb's Up Program" with the actor Melvyn Douglas. This program had a twofold purpose. 1. To encourage support of the

U.S. saving bond drive. 2. To keep up morale for all of our men and women fighting on two fronts.

You moved to Silver Springs, Maryland, just a few miles from the Capitol. The house you rented is really cool and is owned by a Brigadier General in the Air Force who is away stationed in England. Gregory Peck played his story in a movie called, "12O'Clock High". Up in the attic you find some real treasures, hundreds of comic books and all kinds of air force medals and captain bars, wings, etc. You spend a lot of time up there reading to your little heart's content. You are in the 5th grade and the school is located straight down a hill near to your house. You are able slide ride all the way down the hill to your school. What a gas.

One day a lad of similar age comes over to play. He says his name is Bumble and he lives nearby. You become great friends with some real adventures. The following really was something to share and so let's do it.

First of all, we went over to his house which was located not too far away. It was a very large colonial three-story dwelling. Set off the beaten path and pretty much all to itself. Inside you go into a very large room which had several volumes of law books in bookcases. I turn to Bumble and asked, "Is your father a lawyer"? He replied, "He is a Supreme Court Justice". Wow, being very impressed we go on a tour of the house. Up in the attic there are several hams hanging from the rafters. You see several pictures of the Justice in blue jeans and wearing a cowboy hat. He appeared to be a real outdoorsman who loved to explore by hiking and climbing mountains. You are really in awe.

One day the two of you are lying on the grass near the thruway, gazing up into the sky. A feeling of anticipation of what the future has in store for the two of you is felt. Right at this moment you remember it as the first time you began to be thinking about girls and when and who you might get involved with.

The two of you make a raft and try it out on a small stream nearby. It really does not work too well but it was fun. Later you are invited to have dinner with the family. The dining room is very spacious. Present are Moi, Bumble, his older sister, his mom and the Justice who is a rugged, wiry, man. His presence is quite impressive and there appears to be steel mixed with compassion in his eye. He is complaining at the table that driving home from the Court today a lady crashed into his car causing some minor damage. She picks the wrong guy to hit.

The meal is served, and you are having trouble with cutting a large heart of lettuce and what happens was kind of embarrassing. Pressing down on the heart it pops up some 2 feet and Moi caught it with my left hand and calmly put in my left-hand pocket . . . No one says a word. Bumble has a smile on his face thou. One day the two of you are shopping in a drug store. Two girls approach Bumble and ask him, "Are you the son of Justice Douglas"? Bumble nodded yes. Apparently, photos of his children have been shown frequently in the Local Media.

Later that day we stayed out later than usual to be on the street when a test of the Air Raid Alert System is done. Well what happen next was quite surprising. Two men came up to us and say they are with the F.B.I and have been ordered to look for us. Guess staying out too late was not a good idea. P/S I never saw Bumble again. I remained in Maryland for one year and after that returned to l. Benedick Place.

Okay Bubba, "That's better, letting those years come to life is what makes our existence meaningful. It is like looking at a mirror seeing reflections of the choices made gives all a very good idea on how to proceed this day with this wonderful thing called living. Now about those retirement years that had some anxious moments. Well you know I was with you and your lovely through her two hip replacements and you're By Pass Heart Surgery. It was touch and go and when you had all those tubes in ICU after the open-heart operation is when I gave you the idea for this book." "Hey, are you my guardian angel?" "Well look at you. Now 80 years later you finally get it right." "Sorry about that." "Just keep it simple and give back all that love you got over the years." "Amen to that my friend and thanks for taking our Journey." "My pleasure Bubba."

Bubba, I hate to be pest but here's some more of our Journey, that's needs to be told "Okay what is it now?" Well remember when your Mom took you to the World Premier of the, "Wizard of Oz" at Radio City Music Hall and you saw Dorothy in person on the stage and how someone kind of short ran up the aisle with a dozen red roses to give to her. You later found out it was Mickey Rooney. Well you fell in love with that young girl on the stage and later in life as a very young man you met her again at the Sands Hotel and Casino in Las Vegas when she was sitting at the table next to yours with her husband and friends, which included Martha Raye and Peter Lawford You couldn't take your eyes off her and she turned to look at you for a brief moment and gave you one those once in a million smiles that you still hold so secure in your memory. Truly one of those cherish moments.

The next day you are playing the nickel machine at the Sands. Right next to you playing the Silver Dollar Machine is none other than the, "Snooze" also known as Ink a dink a Doo or Jimmy Durante. He works that machine for at least 2 hours, and it is your plan to take the two silver dollars you have in your pocket and play that machine when he is finished Finally, he says, "dats enough." and walks away. So, I prepare to move to machine but at the last minute you are pushed away by a very large hombre in cowboy hat and guess what on the third try, he hits the grand jackpot. What a gas. Several thousand dollars are the prize.

Now your first crush was with another child star. Her name was Joyce Van Patten and she is your first childhood date. You met her through a friend of your Mother. Joyce was at that time on Broadway in a Play called, "Tomorrow the World" About a young German nationalist staying with an American Family during the Second World War. For several months you could think of nothing but her. The first puppy love is quite strong and vital. Truly a great memory and one to cherish. Her career was quite a success doing several movies and TV. shows. Sadly, you did not keep in touch throughout the years.

What seems to be a pattern is your occasional encounters with show business people during our Journey. Later while attending college it happens again when you become a Good Humor Man. Driving an ice cream truck out of Oceanside, Long Island The manager calls you over one day and asks you if you would take an assistant with you on the truck. You say, "No problem."

Well you are really surprised when a midget is introduced to you. He lives nearby with Mr. Olsen of Olsen and Johnson a comedy team which is famous for Hellzapopping. A T V and Broadway show during the late 40's and early 50's. Your helper's role in these shows to enter the stage running very fast with a large paddle which he would wack whoever he could. You say you can still see that as it was yesterday. Funny what one recalls in their twilight years You spend a delightful summer with him. He tells you many stories of his life as part of that comedy team. What a gas.

Later in life three of your Goofers are actors. One is a Brit playing commercials and some movie parts. One is famous for being on the Brit Show called Coronation Street for at least 27 years. Another is an American and will currently be appearing in, Guys and Dolls early next year. A most of all the one and only Mickey D who is a legend in his own time. Mickey celebrated his 102-birthday last Month and is still goofing on a regular basis at the Link's in Hudson, Fla. You 'I never find a finer gentleman playing the Best Game Known to Man. We wish for him many more rounds of goof, Under the Palm Tree. He is truly an inspiration to us all.

Well my readers that's it finally no more memories at this time but don't give up on Moi. Please stay tuned if you can and most important remember we all have a story to tell so pick up that pen and get going.

No time like the present. Stay well and enjoy this wonderful thing called living. With Love, Paulie the Bailie.

Hey Bubba, Put this in your book. "What's that"? Goofing at Black Diamond, in Lecanto, Fla. The drive into the property was the first clue to what kind of day it would be. Perfectly maintained grounds, with shrubs trimmed neatly to a tee. Flowers blooming and very. unique and distinct houses lined the road. Each had their own individual design. The club house was immense with a 100-foot ceiling and large fireplace was viewed in the restaurant. The staff was gracious with smiles galore. But the best was yet to come. What can be said about this layout? Beautiful, outstanding, scrumptious, to say the least. The greens without a doubt the best ever. True as can be. As the putter rolled the ball it hugged the grass like a glove, arching deftly to the hole. dropping in more times than not. "What a Gas, Bubba". Now starting at hole 14 (Quarry Holes) Severe drops down to the holes with the greens chiseled into the landscape causing one to look in awe and many cries of delight were heard. Good shots are required with ample reward when the swing is good and true. Bubba, I watched your swing on that fantastic hole number 17 measuring some 140 yards down a narrow chute surrounded by two high cliffs on each side of the fairway. Those cliffs had to be about 110 yards in height each. I knew as soon as you swung the shot would be good. The sound at impact was loud and clear. The ball arched in high trajectory on a perfect line bouncing near the slight incline that surrounds the hole. The ball nestled and stopped some 6 feet from the hole, but it left a treacherous down hiller which has always been your nemesis. I saw a sudden calmness in your putter's takeaway and you barely hit the putt. It arched down the hill and the green being true kept the ball dead on line as it curled into the hole. I heard you scream, "It's in the hole", and your partners said, "Well done ole man". A fine finale for this tremendous round of Goof. All thought the lesson here is loud and clear. Get out and play this course at least once a year. "That's a direct order Bubba". From Under the Palm Tree, Paulie the Bailie.

For my readers I have 6 footnotes to share. Our story, "Under the Palm Tree", is an ongoing living saga. One can only marvel at some of the events during the past five years that have shaped our destiny. These accounts are mainly one of an observant and not politically motivated. So, I thought important to write to my lead character in my story Bubha as, "Letter's to Bubba". Hoping to bring some credit to those who deserve. It as it has been a real gas of a ride with many up and downs but on a whole very inspiring.

Letter Number One

    Dear Bubba,

Your phone call recently to Moi concerning all the problems facing our country and your utter despair with who is winning the war of words with the far right, needs some clarification. Our country has endured similar discourse many times in the past. For instance, Father Coughlin in the Thirties, Joe McCarthy in the Fifties, The John Birch Society in the Sixtieths, Ted Cruz currently and the list goes on and on. Saner minds prevailed then and there is no reason to think it won't happen again here. Social Security passed after many false accusations calling it Socialism and the ruination of our American Values Of course was proved false and the complete success of this program is now accepted by those right winger's. You might say, it different now with all those billionaires backing those on the far right. Well let's look at another time of chaos and uncertainty when slave owners in the year of our lord 1841 were making huge profits off slaves who were the property of their owners through no fault of their own. Stolen from their homes in Africa and separated from their love one's was so aptly depicted in the current film by Steve McQueen's "12 Years a Slave". This film is truly one of epic portions putting the audience through that horrendous treatment of debauchery and sadistic control over another human being.

Although Mr. McQueen shows these actions in vivid detail with Solomon the main character in the film, the character never loses his self-respect and holds his dignity for all to see. Solomon a free, educated man from Saratoga, New York who is kidnapped while performing as a musician and taken in chains to be sold at a slave auction is more than riveting it will mesmerize you and hold you spellbound. Watching this movie is must for every American as it is a history lesson which needs to be told over and over again for every generation to grasp and hold it close. The ending is very special and for Moi inspiring. Solomon went on to write his story which now is so courageously portrayed in this extremely important film. The Human Spirit is of course indomitable and will as in this fine film endure.

Letter Number Two

Dear Bubba,

All the bad reports on the GOP Presidential 2012 campaign is direct result of a Mole in the Romney Camp.

Who was placed for the purpose to cause confusion internal damage which has been manifested quite blatantly of late?

Add this to these past gaffes and you got bingo a Mole alive and well. See below the mole's advice to Gov. Romney.

1. *Tell Gov. Romney if he is attacked for his liberal actions while Gov of Mass. bet them a large sum of money like $10,000 that their accusation is wrong.*
2. *Visit London, England prior to the Olympics and it ask how things are going tell them that the Brits need to take a page out of your book on how to run and get ready for the Games. Mention that it is, "Disconcerting*

on what is happening in England today and for them to ask you for help."

3. Do the blame game on the President on as much as you can for the mess that G.W. got us into. Stretch the truth as much as possible. A few fibs won't hurt just like the Chicken Soup.

4. Get a mystery guest to speak to an empty chair that it is so bizarre and pure lunacy that it raises concerns about the basic mental health of the delegates if they laugh at this.

5. Have some candidates running for the Senate speak to the abortion case that when women are raped, they will not get pregnant. As the brain will release a block to any sperm.

6. Have your Vice President Running mate brag about his running and how fast he ran at marathons even if it is 2 hours off. Who will know? Only the Shadow will know.

7. Visit the hurricane recent damage in La. and if anyone ask you for help, tell them to call a Gov. Agency even give them the exact number 211 for assistance. If you can shed a tear it would be very helpful.

8. Be so blatantly wrong on the facts regarding the recent Libya Embassy that my 8 years Grandson sees it.

9. Attacked the 47% that have no federal income tax. Write them off and concentrate on the 1% at the top for your support.

10. The final message from the Mole is for, "Gov. Romney, at all be yourself."

Letter Number 3

Dear Bubba,

The Farmhouse

Okay Bubba, another memory you need to share is the great times you and family had with your good Buddy, Ken. Redman. It's seems like yesterday that you and your lovely and 2 daughters would without fail go most weekends to Ken's house located on a sod farm in Syosset, Long Island. You told me that you can still smell those German Cookies that were made from the best recipe known to man. Each bite was truly an experience for one's taste buds melting in one's mouth. A real treat that we all still remember.

The many barbecues and picnic's full of fun and games was so perfect that time seemed to stand still. There were many heated discussions in the kitchen where we all tried to solve the many problems facing the world. It was a time our kids grew up knowing their parents were always there for them and in our humble way gave them the ability to grow and prepare themselves for their own separate journey which you told was a complete success for Ken's 3 children and your 2 children. Today they are all well on their journey with hope for the future. They in turn are doing exactly the same for their children.

Now the news came without warning and was truly a shock. Your pal and close friend who stood by you when times personally became hard, helped you so much to regroup and get on with your journey, passed away. What can you say about Ken? For starters. He was a man for the people. A strong believer that all people are created equal and have the right to happiness. He was a great track man. He ran many marathons and I can still see him in his running outfit which he wore proudly. He inspired your daughter Cynthia to run and attended many of her competitors while in High School. Your daughter today still has his words of advice tucked safely away. She continues to run every day sometimes as much as 15 miles early each day. He was faithful husband and dedicated father. He was always true to his convictions and a fine example for family and community.

Now what is truly interesting that for the past several weeks you have been trying to get in touch with him, but the phone number was disconnected, and you mentioned it to your daughter Cynthia who in turn tried to see what was going on. Well that's how you found out Ken passed away quietly in his sleep. You told me that as you wrote this several tears gently fell on your cheeks. So, stop those tears sobbing Bubba and celebrate a great friend's life for what really matters is all the love you got from each other over those terrific years. Amen to that, thanks Bubba.

Letter Number 4

Dear Bubba,

Seldom to we witness a special journalistic piece of reporting as we did last Sunday in the article by Douglas McCollum in Tampa Bay Times Perspective Section. It deserves recognition as one of the finest analysis of our current political environment and is a must reading by all Americans. The comparison of the economic upheavals of the 30/s and period between 2000-2008 of economic turmoil showed us that during these times of crisis some take to the air waves screaming's false and groundless accusations towards those in power, who they think will *destroy this country is example of pure hysteria which goes unchecked can lead to direr consequences in itself. So, when back in*

1930's when Father Coughlin took the airways attacking the New Deal of President Roosevelt, he could have prevented the passage of Social Security and Unemployment Insurance and where would we be today if we did not have these safety nets. I give thanks that saner minds prevailed. As Mr. McCollum points out a lesson to be learned here from those past experiences and the return to rational, intelligent discourse is imperative to deal with these Global problems that confront our Planet today. We are again at a crossroad and we need to take affirmative action to solve them. Listening to those extremists will only delay and muddle the action that is needed. So, let all of those extremist's that are screaming with absurdities stop take a deep breath and sit down and read yes read Mr. McCollum article again and again. Maybe the lesson they learn will calm down their hysteria and we will move forward once again as we did under F.D.R

Letter Number 5

Dear Bubha,

Rarely in our Nation's history do we experience a more defining moment as we all did when Rep. Gabby Gifford's strode into the chambers of the House of Representatives that memorable day to cast her vote on the Debt Ceiling Bill. It was a moment to cherish, to see that display of courage and dedication. From that day forward Ms. Gifford has been on a crusade for sanity in controlling access by sick people to weapons of people destruction. It was extraordinary in that it sends a message to those who wish us harm for our beliefs, which is if you knock us down, we will get up to fight again we will not tolerate those actions and seek proper justice and the freedom to express our beliefs. Our nation's principles are firmly in place and only become stronger when those who wish us harm attack us, but we need to take prompt and decisive measures to keep weapons out of the hands of disturbed individuals. One thing for sure is survival is not a thing of chance but a determination to live which is shared by all well-meaning peoples. For those lackey's who refuse to consider reasonable gun control measures the fight has just begun. We will as a nation will keep plugging away until the fight is won. So, help us God.

Letter 6 to Bubba

Dear Bubba,

Credit must be given to our young pragmatic President who among other positive things ended the war in Iraq and winding down the other one. The casualties have almost completely stopped and military families are being untied to enjoy their time Under the Palm Tree. The Economy is greatly improving, with the Auto Industry Assembly Lines are humming once more. Over 8 million American now have health care. Hey Bubba, how about those 36,000 Boston Marathon runners this year. Honoring the victims of last year's dastardly attack showing to the world that we are united and will not be intimated by these cowardly acts of terror.

Hey Bubba, I must also mention my Lovely, wife, Sigrid of 50 years who being a German Citizen and grew up during WWII in Kassel, Germany, losing her beloved Dad in the war. Her mother kept the family together with pure grit and strength that so many more German's did at that time. Of course, the rest is history as they rebuilt their nation from the ground up to become this day a staunch ally for Democracy.

The other day your Lovely had a freak accident falling from bed and had need to see if her year-old hip replacement was damage in the process. There was lots of pain. So, a decision had to be made who to seek out treatment on this weekend. Where to go? A new hospital to the area was chosen. Trinity E/R located in the rear of the Hospital on State Road 54 was simply fantastic. Your lovely was in a room within 5 minutes. Immediate medical attention was given in very professional and courteous manner. One had the feeling they were at a 5-star resort. What a gas. Something to note for all living in the area

So, there you have it Bubba. Times to reflect and to act. One more thing Bubba, A big thank you to the many great films of 2012-2013 that bring into focus our Nation's Culture, Hopes and Aspirations. To name a few: Nebraska, 12 Years a Slave, The Texas Buyer's Club, Captain Phillips, and Lincoln.

Hope is a contagious thing, bringing us closer to our love ones. Every moment we share this with family and friends, is truly something to hold and grab every moment to keep these glorious memories close, as we make our life's journey.

It's the dawn of revitalization and rebirth of our Nation's principles and strength. Hopefully our Nation's voter's will place supportive Rep's to continue this journey. So long for now Bubba, I stay as always, your obedient servant.

THE OPERATION

Hey Bubba, our journey had some tough going with some health issues that many Senior's face as they make their own separate journey's. So, let's give it a go and share what happened. It could be of some interest to many Seniors who may have similar issues as they make their own separate trek through the Golden Years of Retirement.

The year is 2003 you and your lovely are firmly in place in your living in Hudson, Fla. It has been almost 10 years since the move from the hustle and bustle of New York. Your health has been under the watchful eye of the Bayonet Point Cardiology Associates Group, under the care of Dr. J. Nareddy. For the past 9 years you have been seeing them and they finally persuade you to have your irregular heart beat checked out. This condition has been a real pain since the late 90's. Causing anxiety and worry that all is not well.

The cauterization was done where dye is injected into you blood stream and view on a T.V. Screen for any obstruction and blockages. Well the results are truly alarming. One artery is totally block and 3 others are more than 50% blocked. A surgeon pokes his head in through the testing site and says, "We need to operate immediately. How about tomorrow morning". I remember you saying, "Can I think about it". The young Surgeon said, "Not a good idea as it is life threatening". He explains the need to take fast and direct action. Well Bubba, I had to whisper in your ear, "Go for it. I'll be with you and we will make it through".

They send you home with an order to not drink or eat anything and return to Building D at 6PM this day.

After checking in you are taken to the basement and prepared for the early AM open heart operation. The attendant is helpful and asked, "Do you need something to help you sleep". I remember you saying, "Nah". So off to bed you go. It is dark and dreary, and you toss and turn, and several strange images come into your head. Something out of Monster Movie. You're in a long dark tunnel with glaring images stalking you at every turn. I hear you say drats and ugh this is not going to work. So, I tell you go see the attendant and get something. Well it worked the next you know you are being wheeled into the O/R. The last thing you remember is the bright lights overhead.

Now something is very funny about how you feel no anxiety and you are completely relaxed. Must have been some pretty good stuff they gave you or maybe it because I am with you Bubba.

The next thing you know you awakened and asked, "Where am I". The reply is "you just had an operation". Wow you just lost 6 hours. Like those minutes never happen. You noticed there are several tubes attached to your bod. A nurse comes to check you and at once you feel her kind and thoughtful caring towards you, Truly a very kindred relationship develops. You noticed that she walks with a limp which does not prevent the exceptional care that was provided. Funny within just a few minutes and very strong bond of friendship builds.

I see this Bubba and immediate realize that this is a rare person that one occasionally meets in life and is instantly seen as a blessing. This rare encounter and unselfish attention should be recognized with gratitude. So, what you do is very interesting. I had told you about a new Company that is going by the stock symbol ONXX that was currently selling around $4. You tell her about it saying, "Something to look into for your future my friend". She replies, "Are you giving me a stock tip" You heard a reply," That is an affirmative". Not knowing if this was acted upon, one can only hope that she did. For this stock topped out recently for $124. per share and was the best rewarding stock pick for 2013. This kind soul maybe the better for it. We certainly hope so.

Well in three months your back in the swing. Your golf has never been better. The great thrill on the course is about to happen. In 2013 while playing in one of your Tournaments at the Link's Saturday Shoot Out.

A hole in one. It's the fourth in 70 years of Goofing for you Bubba and I think I had a hand in that as well. What a gas. When approaching the hole, the ball was clearly resting inside the hole. A shot for all ages. A truly thrilling and wonderful feeling. You came a long way for that Bubba.

Golf again proves that playing this game keeps one young in more ways than one. It is only fitting that the day before writing this, you again meet up with Mickey D now heading for 101 years of age. He just arrived last week from Buffalo and is back playing Goof at the Link's in Hudson Fla. You gave him a big hug. And shared some thoughts on this great game. I can only wish for Mickey many more rounds of the Greatest Game Known to Man.

So, there you have it. There are some detours one must face while making their life's journey. Taking chances and trusting those who can help you is not a matter of chance but a defined destiny we all have on this swirling planet. Stay well my readers and have a super, great Journey of your own and don't forget everyone has a story to tell so pick up that pen and get to work. You are proud to announce that your 12-year-old Granddaughter Elizabeth is doing just that. During your second Daughter Jennifer's last visit, Elizabeth wrote a really sweet little story about a miss understood child who gets accused of something she did not do. The story has a great ending and shows lots of promise for more stories by her in the foreseeable future. So, write on my young lady and bring forth all of that wonderful imagination that you are so lucky to have, That's goes for all you other Bubba' out there too. Your life is story to be told. From Under the Palm Tree . . . Paulie the Ballie

THE STRAY

Well now, its 2004, and it has been one year since the Operation. Your life has pretty much settled down, Bubba. So, what happens next is something that warms the heart.

You have always had a dog through childhood on Long Island, Kansas, and now in Florida. The companionship that those beloved pets provide is something to cherish. They are always loyal and offer unconditional love. When you come home a grand welcome is always offered. The tails are constantly wagging with joy.

So, when a large tri color hound dog is found in your neighborhood, you recognize immediately as a stray. She is not shy at all and comes right up to you with enthusiasm and trust.

Your Lovely permits the animal into your house. You both contemplate on what do to. So, we keep the dog for now to think about it.

The next day you both need to go to the store. Thinking it is not a good idea to leave the dog in the house as the animal constantly romps several laps threw the house having a ball. So, we decide to leave her outside in our screen patio. When we return, we find a large hole in the screening and according a neighbor she never left the yard and is waiting for us to return. You think to yourself Bubba, looks like we got a pet.

Well something happens that is very strange. Destiny strikes again. A German family who have rented a house down the block for a few weeks, have taken an interest in the dog as their three young children simply adore her. So, your Lovely who also German talks to them and a plan is made.

The family will take the animal but here's the catch, International laws prevent the travel out of the country without a 30-day waiting period after all the shots have been administered and have been certified fit to travel. So, your Lovely agreed to tend to all of the documentation as the family is going home the day after tomorrow. Sure, enough all goes well. The 30 days fly by and we on our way to the airport with the dog in the traveling cage, ready for the flight to her new home in Germany. When checking in the cargo attendant says there is no name on the manifesto, and he would need to have one. So, your Lovely says, "Lets name her Lucky". Wow, that's a winner, perfect I say. So Lucky it is. I hear you say Bubba, "Have a great flight Lucky and be happy".

One week later we received a letter from Germany. All went well and Lucky is doing just fine. Still romping in the large fenced yard. Every year at Christmas we received a card with picture of a very happy Lucky. This goes on for ten long years until Lucky peacefully dies in her sleep. We both shed a tear when the news arrives. However, resting assured that those ten years were filled with love and caring for a very lucky stray. Knowing that there are many more Lucky's waiting for a home. So, visit that your local Pound and bring home your best pal. Take it from me Bubba it will be a gas. From Under the Palm Tree My Hoppy says good idea Pilgrim.

Author resting with his faithful dog Hoppy.

THE BATTLE OF CHANCELLORSVILLE

Well now, a little background on this bloodiest battle of the Civil War (4/27/1863-5/6/1863) This battle for both sides was a travesty of immense proportions. The union army lost 1,606 killed and 9,672 wounded and 5,919 captured. The Army of North Virginia last 1,665 killed and 9,081 wounded and 2,018 captured or missing.

A total of three Union Generals were killed and more notably for the South, Stonewall Jackson and Brig General Elisha F. Patton. A terrible loss for The Confederacy who Longstreet said could not afford to lose.

The New York Tribune reporter, Horace Greeley, call it, "My God it is horrible-horrible, and to think of it 133,000 magnificent soldiers so cut to pieces by less than 60,000 half- starved ragamuffins".

Well, Bubba, your Great Grand Pappy was there fighting as a young Union Solider from Missouri. Here is a little of what He told me what happen, as he kept a journal.

My name is William Harrison Spidell, I am 20 years old and this is my first time in battle. We have been positioned in a tree lined area with our cannons pointing towards the open field ahead. The area is called Spotsylvania County, Virginia. I am German and English descent and was raised on a small farm in Missouri. I answered the call for duty and enlisted two months before.

As I lie here waiting, I hear some crickets and watch some birds high above soaring away. One can only marvel on how quiet it is. I wonder how I will behave when the bullets start to fly and have some anxious moments but try to remember the wise counsel, I got from my commanding officer who said when the battle is on one will be so busy loading and reloading there will no time to be afraid. So, put aside those fears young man as what will be will be. He goes on to say what we are fighting for is the very survival of our Nation. Our forefathers gave us a Constitution that is worth trying to preserve and this war must be won to achieve that end. No man should be the master of another. No man should enslave and debased and dehumanized another. Seldom in recorded history has such a principle been defended for some many peoples. At that very moment you hear a tremendous roar directly in front of you and immediately recognized as thousand voices yelling at the top of their voices It is hard to discerned what it is, but you think it's, "Here comes Stonewall"

You hear the command Fire at Will, Fire at Will, your hands are calm, and the reloading goes well for at least 12 shots are done before you feel a great force hit your leg. You look down at the bone is sticking out and the blood is gushing forth. The bandanna Mom gave you comes in handy and the medic uses it to apply a tourniquet. Now Bubba getting hit like this so early in the campaign is truly a blessing for you are taken off the front lines to the rear and taken for transport to hospital to save that leg.

The battle rages on for 6 days and the Union is defeated and General Lee's uses daring tactics by splitting his forces into two forks of assault and causes a wedge in the Union Positions. The Union General concedes and withdraws. Critics will later call him too timid and unwilling to counter attack.

But History tells us although the South had a major victory here, they were mortally wounded losing too many soldiers in the process and the loss of Stonewall Jackson was catastrophic.

Now what happens just one week later when still resting in Hospital is truly amazing. It is early one morning you look up and see a tall figure approaching your bed. His face is something you will never forget.

Gaunt but with a very determined look in his eye. He comes to your bed and extends his hand. You grab it and a strange calmness radiates forth. You know at once President Lincoln is smiling at you. He says, "Young man your sacrifice here will not be in vain. What you have done here, fighting to preserve this great nation will resonate throughout time. Your children and their children will be forever grateful for you and all the other young men actions here. Our task is not an easy one and but one that must be done. Freedom for all no matter what color they may be is what we are fighting for. And some day a man of color may be holding this office as I do this day. God bless you and thank you for your service to this great Nation".

Well you get sent home wounded and unfit for further duty. In two more years, the War will be done. You find a Lovely and get married and have 4 children of which one is this Author's Grandfather. Now want to hear something that is a real gas, This Author's Daughter, Cynthia has a son and not knowing about you Great Pappy gives him your middle name, that being Harrison. Wow some defined destiny again Bubba. From Under the Palm Tree

A TALE OF TWO PINS

This is the story of the remarkable Pin, called a, "Safety Pin". A young American man, named Walter Hunt in the year of our Lord 1849, had a debt of $15 owed to a very pervasive man who was constantly at him for payment. Well, now it motivated him to think of inventing something that he could sell in order to settle that persistent creditor constant nagging for payment.

So, he got two wires together with sort of clasp at one end to work as a spring like action with an enclosed end which remarkably held the end of pin firmly in place after engagement. He thought he could sell it and so he approached a representative of the W.R. Grace Company and bingo he was offered $400 on the spot. He signed the release immediately and paid off that debt giving him $385, a small fortune for our young inventor.

It was a fantastic deal for W.R. Grace as they were to reap millions off this remarkable pin which could be used to safely hold diapers in place for millions of newborns and many other uses for every household.

Unfortunately for Mr. Hunt, he never thought to asked for a share of the profits for his invention and never saw another dime.

Well by now you may be asking what has this got to do with life Under the Palm Tree? So, here's what happened. Recently this Author and his Lovely took a cruise on Holland American on the Ryndam, departing from the Tampa Port. Parking is very convenient right next to the boat within a 300-yard drive to the entrance. During that cruise your Lovely took part in a 5 K walk on board for Cancer with two new hips'. You proud to say she was successful in completing the walk and several hundred dollars were raised.

PAULIE THE BALLIE

Wow that's really cool for an 82-year-old Grandma. Hey Bubba, you only lasted for one lap around the boat. The spirit was willing, but the body was not. This ship is truly an elegant antique and sadly will be retired sometime this year. A new ship is in the works. What was extraordinary were the number of passengers that had disabilities requiring them to use walker's for moving about the ship. This seemed not to worry any of them, and a good time was had by all.

One of our dinner companions, a couple from New Hampshire took a side trip on a river boat in the heartland of Guatemala to see the effects of their Rotary Club's charitable assistance. Their efforts were enabling the locals to purchase water filters to purify the water which was unsafe to drink without this much needed treatment. They were thrilled to see that those efforts were having a very positive result's and were greatly appreciated. Truly a noble cause.

Hoppy your faithful dog had just been left with his dog sitter on the way to the ship Hoppy had a large fenced yard to roam and seemed to love it there.

The cruise flew by and seven days later we arrived back in Tampa. After disembarking we went directly to the sitter to pick up Hoppy. He seemed happy to see us and appeared to be okay.

Later that night he began to howl and became quite agitated. Wow, what's going on? The next day this continued and a call to the Vet. Was done. Hoppy was immediately examined by Dr. Garrison, of Spring Hill. Dr. Garrison took an x-ray of his tummy and immediately came to us and said, "Please you have to see this". The x-ray revealed two small safety pins in the exact middle of his stomach. The good news that they were both firmly closed and with any luck could be passed out as waste. This could take up to another week, however. After 8 days, we notice some improvement but there was still some occasional howling. So back to the Vet. For another look.

Well, nothing was found, and the Dr. said he passed it. So, folks that pin lived up to its name and a big thank you to Mr. Walter Hunt for he amazing invention.

Several weeks later, We had to switch Vet. services for Hoppy. His tail was strangely quiet, and his weight began to diminish. Plenty of water drinking and frequent urination. Then some serious problems occurred when he began to constantly to throw up and stopped eating. I became quite anxious, so I told you do something Bubba. Hoppy needs immediate medical attention. So, you called the emergency number which referred you to the Animal Emergency Clinic on State Road 19 in New Port Rickey. He was examined and the diagnosis was Diabetes, requiring hospitalization to bring down that extremely high blood sugar number. Dr Lee attended, and his prognosis was encouraging as it was a condition that can be treated. Hoppy will required constant monitoring however with a special diet and injections of insulin

His condition showed a marked improvement and after two days he was discharged to you Bubba and your Lovely. You take him home and later that day it is time for his injection. That first injection was quite a trip as the needle got your middle finger and a small dose of insulin was released. You feel a little strange for a moment, but it quickly passes and bingo your second try was a success. You are happy to report Hoppy's tail is again wagging and he is getting into trouble again. His constant search for food is back.

Hopefully he will be okay and thanks for that quick decision for help. Having this playful pet for so many years has been a delightful experience and with good care he should be okay so we can continue together as one family Under the Palm Tree. We all say, "Phew that was close".

THE CHOICE

*T*his story is based on true events. The names have been changed to protect privacy.

Okay it is the year of our Lord 1964. Your Lovely is working for a German Food Processing Machine Company on the North Shore of Long Island. Here the machines are assembled after being shipped from Germany. The office has a small staff of 6 including the Manager and your Lovely who runs the clerical side of the business.

After about 6 months a young girl from Germany comes to help out in the Office. Her name will be Erika and she hopes to stay for at least a year or two. We become friends with Erika, and we have an active social life. Taking small trips to New England and seeing some Broadway Shows. A great time is had by all.

One day Erika confides that she is pregnant, and her child is due in 5 months. She and the father had discussed their options and since the father was a married man and refusing to leave his family, the following was up for a decision. 1. An abortion done in Switzerland. 2. Take a transfer to the U.S.A. Office and have the baby and put the child up for adoption. 3. Keep the child and continue to work after a few months and put the baby in a suitable day care situation.

Knowing this was Erika's decision alone no real advice was given. However, we offered our support to whatever she decided to do. Well option 2. was done and the birth of child went well a beautiful blonde-haired baby girl was born.

The adoption went well, and Erika returned to Germany shortly thereafter.

Years later we heard she had married, and we never heard from her again.

Many years later a young mother of two went searching for her biological mother as many adoptee's are doing now. Information from the Agency was obtained and an address in Germany was found. A trip was planned for a reunion of sorts. The young Mother was anxious to find out all she could. Well Ericka was still alive living in a Nursing Home outside of Frankfurt

A knock on the door and a voice said, "come in please". The young mother ventured into the room and found a graying hair woman in her 70" s sitting in an arm chair. In that moment a sudden recognition was experienced by both. The young mother ran to hug that women with a sudden sense of freedom. The old lady was crying softly and as they were hugging the old lady looked over the young women's shoulder and saw two youngsters holding on their mother's skirt. Suddenly several doors were flunged wide open and a tremendous feeling of joy was felt by Mother and Daughter. The years melted away and this moment was truly a time to never forget. And if one listen real close you could hear the young mother's words, "Thank you Omi."

The twins would visit each year for the rest of Erika's life learning to speak German and ski the many slopes of Europe.

THE TORCH

What fool's gamut do these Pols play?
Building walls of hate each day
No thought given to Emma Lazarus famous words.
"Give me your tired, your poor, your huddled masses
yearning to breathe free,
The wretched refuse of your teeming shore.
Send these, the homeless, tempest-tost to me,
I lift my lamp beside the golden door!"
So, spread the word least one forgets
what our Nation's was founded for.
One thing for sure Our Lady's Torch is burning
brightly this day and is here to stay and will endure.
From Under the Palm Tree

THE TRIP

Hey Bubba, what about that extraordinary trip by the Pope. What did you take away from his visit? Well for starters it was a call for Universal Decency. With all the problems going on in the world it is so necessary to show that this Nation will fulfill its credo and to see that we will not be deterred from accomplishing that goal by taking the lead and giving the solace and refuge to many disenfranchise that need to breathe free air and have a chance and an opportunity to pursue a life without fear.

His Holiness was putting us on alert to take action. His powerful message was strong and true. It was like a breath of fresh air blowing away the confusion and clearing a path to walk down. Millions heard this message and it is now up to our Pols to decide what direction to take. Hopefully they will put away self-glorification and serve the people with whom they were required to do when being sworn ed in. The ball is now in their hands. One thing they should think about is what kind of legacy they will record and how helpful were their actions to follow the Pope's vital message. "Do unto others what you want them to do to you". It was a great message giving hope to the World. A magical time with each moment a time of celebration of the goodness that is in all well-meaning peoples.

Hey Bubba, can I say something? "Sure, fire away". "Life maybe unique in our Galaxy and maybe the Universe. This swirling planet maybe an experiment to see if Humanity can survive here before it is permitted to occur elsewhere in the Solar System. So, let's not fail in our endeavor.

Keep it simple and let's not forget the Holy Father's Message".

Recently there have been some more promising developments that we can be thankful for. 1. The recent medical report on the success in treating Parkinson and possibly Alzheimer's with a new drug called, "Nilotinib". It could be a God send to millions of those who suffer from those aliments, 2. In the November and December Issue of Publication Mother Jones we have a Pulitzer Prize Candidate with an in-depth study of the Mass Shooting's that have become all too frequent of late. The message is simple.

Every American needs to be diligent and on the lookout for warning signs of potential attacks by being ever watchful and report these alarming behaviors to the authorities for intervention. Several examples of previous perpetrators are discussed and examined. Truly a masterful study of the serious phenomenon that is killing far too many. Okay Bubba that's about it.

Hope is on the rise and one should be made aware of the good that is done by the countless kind souls who come into the fray to help the fallen and down- trodden. Our Motto, "We can do it yes we can".

THE COLLABORATORS

Perception as defined in the dictionary is the way you think about or understand someone or something. In addition, it is the act or faculty of perceiving or apprehending by means of the senses or of the mind, cognition understanding.

We all have to make choices based on our perception of the matter confronting us.

How we make these decisions pretty much determines what path we will take. So, the ability to make the best possible decisions is of course determined by how accurate these perceptions are and once made how they will affect your life's journey.

Not all peoples have the same perception on things such as politics', religion, truth, etc. These differences are so evident in our current political debate. One must be so careful on what is based on fact and not false assertions that play on fear and hate. Of course, all have the right to express their views, but the real danger lies in electing those extremist's to office such as we see is currently on display in the Republican race for the White House. In my following short story titled, "The Collaborators" I have in Chapter One, "The Encounter", brought two brilliant minds of literature and the Cinema together during a chance meeting on a train in Essex, England in the year of Our Lord 1925 They both are prime examples of using peoples different perceptions to create stories with countless surprises that we all have cherished over the years.

I have no evidence to prove they ever had this meeting but who is to deny it could have happened. Both are English, both are within seven years of age of each other. Our Heroine is 7 years younger than our Hero. She comes from a family of artists and her father was an actor of some note, Gerald du Maurier. Her sister Angela also was a writer. Her Grandfather was the artist and writer George du Maurier. What a background for this brilliant writer. Daphne du Maurier

Now to our Hero, a young man on the move. He became interested in his life's vocation at a very young age. He wrote his first story in 1919 about a young woman who has a hallucination about being assaulted. He would go on the write several more stories with diverse subjects. Shortly thereafter he became interested in Photography and started working in film production. He had a five-year apprenticeship and got his first film director job. He would go on to be one the greatest film directors of the 20th century. He is often referred as the, "Master of Suspense" You probably already guessed his name, my personal hero, Alfred Hitchcock. Now to the Meeting

THE ENCOUNTER

She was on her way to visit her family in London, The train ride from Essex only took 60 minutes so no one thought she couldn't do it on her own. Her appearance was striking, Beautiful light brown hair that form a somewhat tassel of light when the sun hit it. She was dressed in a traditional suit of light brown color. She was deeply engrossed in her book, When the young man came into the compartment. He was slightly overweight. But no one would call him fat. There was an air of a confident person who was ever watchful of the wonders about him. One could see he was very observant and storing much of his experiences safely away for future reference. He noticed the young women at once and thought to himself wow what an interesting face. Their eyes locked for a brief moment and the young man had the strangest feeling they met once before. His interest was so strong he could not refrain from introducing himself. To his amazement she extended her hand saying hello. He immediately exchanged the greeting saying something about how great the weather was for this time of the year. She smiled and at that moment a bond of friendship occurred. They would talk of all sorts of things during next hour. He hadn't talked to anyone like this during his life. She told him about her writings, and he mentioned his stories as well. Both were extremely interested in what the other had to say. It was one of those magical moments. Right then a pact was made by these two young artists to keep a watchful eye out for their future works and just maybe they would someday collaborate. And the rest is history they would do 3 films together that become classic tales of mystery and intrigue. Rebecca, Jamaica Inn, and The Birds.

What they both shared was the knowledge that the human condition could take violent turns without warnings. These occurrences could happen at any time and to anyone. People of ordinary lives were not immune. How some survived these twists of fate runs rampant through both of their respective works.

Both were saddened when the train pulled into the London Terminal. They parted as friends for life and would go their separate ways. Daphne to a marriage with three children to military hero of WWII. And Alfred to marry his Alma his love of his life who would aide him so well with his film's success. Truly one of the great collaborations of all time.

One may ask what this has do with life Under the Palm Tree. Well we all had a long hard journey to get there. Our perceptions played an enormous role in what choices we had to make to get here. I tried to explore this in my real-life story titled "The Choice", of young women who decided to go full term with her pregnancy and give life to her daughter who years later she will meet.

Now the big questions how we can protect this Retirement and not lose what we worked so hard for., For the past eight years we have seen economic progress and the unemployment rate has dropped to an 8-year low. People are shopping once more, and the stock market is booming. Some say 2016 will be a banner year for stocks. Making the right choices on who we elected to guide this Nation so that we can continue this progress is imperative. Think it out my friend and I am confident you will make the right choice so we all can say, "Another Day in Paradise".

God Bless from Under The Palm Tree.

THE GAME

Crunch, Swish, down the fairway it goes

Stroke a spinning roll Straight to the hole

A plunk you hear like gold.

Game for all to behold

Ups and downs for sure

Much like Life

A detour or two

But always back for more

As we mosey to distant shore

One is heard to say FORE

THE FEELING

Hey Bubba, what now? Well for starters, We need a moment of silence for the passing of our good friend and golfer, Mickey D. He played this great game right to the end of his 102 years. We will solely miss his inspirational golfing skills. He never spoke an unkind word. He was a jolly and positive presence on the golf course. Several months ago, I and my Lovely ran into Mickey D in a local favorite cafe the Oaks, in Hudson, Fla. We had a delightful talk about golf. Seizing on the moment, I poised to Mickey a question about the golf swing that I have been searching for the past 70 years. It was, "What is the one thing you think about when starting the golf swing"? As I waited in eager anticipation for the answer, Mickey replied, "Nothing at all". I thought about this, and by gosh he is right. The swing is just under 3 seconds and there is no time to be thinking about the several swing thoughts you have been given over the years. So, I tried it and without any noticeable improvements I went one step further and added this. One needs to not think but have the following which is a feeling. As you start the back swing have both hands working together without any tension, keeping this feeling throughout the back swing and down swing. This relax motion will keep the club in the best position to hit the ball square and flush. Any tension in the hands is a rhythm inhibitor and must not occur at any time during the swing. Have your palms facing each other with a neutral grip. So, let it fly and bingo down the middle of the fairway it goes. Hey Bubba. What now. When I was checking in Upstairs, I ran into Mickey D, who was heading to the first tee to play with his new foursome. Wow, that's great who is he paired with? Oh. He said their names are: Ike, and Bobby and Payne. He got four shots a nine. Have fun My friend. We miss you. Here are some suggestions if one is visiting this haven of the most affordable goof in the good ole U.S.A Tell them Paulie the Ballie sent ya. and play well.

1. *Silverthorn, Brooksville, Fla;*
2. *The Eagles, Odessa Fla*
3. *World Woods, Brooksville Fla*

THE BALLADEER

It's truly a rare bird

That sings her song

To make it right

What is so wrong

Always true for us to see

The way that is best for thee

So sing on and on to help

Us navigate these turbulent Seas

All the best Ms. J.B and be of good cheer

This your 75th year.

EPILOGUE!!!

The debate of what constitutes literature continues. The official definition is a foreground of poetic effects. It is this literalistic or poeticity of literature that distinguishes it from ordinary speech or other kinds of writings. This official definition is far too limited. Literature embodies the very culture that it sprang from. Each generation has it's form of literature of its time. As that period represents what perils and fortunes that occurred during that time span. Literature explains those events in precise and definite terms. Without this generational literature; we would have no sense of who we are or whom we want to become. Literature of the times is a tool of passing on to future generations the culture and accomplishments and dreams that were held during those periods which must be held close least we forget to learn from them.

"Wow that was a mouthful Bubba". "Oh, stop it and use that brain Silly and pick up that pen-e- and write your story today". From Under The Palm Tree.

AFTERMATH LAMENT

As more shooting of innocents comes our way
Will something finally be done this day?
As this Congress refuses to have a say.
What to do with this dismay?
All need to vote this election day
And remove these lackeys of the N.R.A
Take them to task for failure to act
Send them packing in disgrace that hardened pack
For dereliction of duty of the oath they were sworn to say
So, let's get to the polls this election day
And cast that vote to let the word go forth
We want a change to take these weapons off our streets
At last saving lives and setting a better example for the World
That we are at last a Nation of preserving life
And that all have a right
To pursue their lives without fear
Of a random act of violence and hate
From Under The Palm Tree

THIS ELECTION

Dear Bubba,

What now? Well I am scared. What do you mean? Well for starters, We have a very important choice on who will be our next President. On one hand we have a talented woman with many years of experience in dealing with a very turbulent events on a global scale. On the other hand, we have a bombastic candidate in Donald Trump. He does not appear to have a good grasp on the dangers facing our Nation and the need to have as many allies as possible to help maintain world stability and peace. His failure to take Nuclear Weapons off the table is frightening. These weapons can never be used. If they were used, we may see the end to humanity. Our planet could be literally blown apart. Killing countless millions of peoples. We must have a steady hand at the helm. We must remove all of these weapons from every arsenal period. Not threaten to use them.

Withdrawing from the World Community is very similar to our Nation's failure to commit to the League of Nations back shortly after the World War I. Our lack of attendance and support doomed the League of Nations at the Paris Conference and planted the seeds for the World War II. Some historians acknowledge that our isolation then was one of the contributing factors and if we had indeed followed Woodrow Wilson's 14 Points both Germany and Japan could not have armed themselves to attack and that horrendous war would have been prevented. Oh, to go back in time and whisper in the ears of Senator Henry Cabot Lodge and President Harding. Can we at last learn from the past or will we stumble and make a huge mistake we did those many years gone past? Well Bubba, there you have it. I pray to God our country will make the right decision for our children's sake. From Under The Palm Tree.by Paulie the Ballie

THANK YOU

Bubba and I want to take a pause to say something that needs to be said now!

The extraordinary speech by Khizr Khan with his lovely wife at his side, at the Democratic Convention showed to the world that this Country is a diverse one without exceptions. Those words were without a doubt were a beacon of light which had truly an electrifying significance for the world in general. It sent a message to all well-meaning peoples that we are on a mission to make this swirling planet a better and safer place. It could change those darken hearts of the far right and maybe the mind set of those many terrorists that think of us as enemies to be attack by killing countless innocents at will. Maybe we get at last get reasonable gun control passed. Maybe we can reassure the world we will fight terrorist aggression on all fronts until it is stopped once and for all the killing of some many innocent peoples.

A personal message to the Madam Khan and Mr. Khan, I want to express our profound thank you for your son's service to our Country. His willingness to give his life to his country to protect all free peoples will resonate through time. We are in war of survival and his actions there in the far away land will never be forgotten. Thank you and we can only pray your grief for him will have kind memories of the many years he spent with you as a youngster. The fine qualities that you both instilled in him gave him so much. That he had the courage to fight for all our freedoms. Thank you, thank you, thank you, I hope all the best for your family during this time of grief and if you don't to talk about it so be it. The mother's love for her son is the strongest force on earth.

This love will endure as long as there is life here. I have written a poem for you. **Our Son**

> *His broad smile when he rode that bike for the first time*
> *His laughter when he passed that drivers test.*
> *His look of thank you when he got the car for the first date*
> *His hug when he graduated from school that day.*
> *His knowledge you were there for him no matter what*
> *These memories will never be forgotten and will always last.*
> *Thank you so much we all are in your debt.*

1907

The year is 1907, and why my friend is this important year to remember now?

Well for starters it is the first of back to back wins by the Chicago Cubs in the World Series of Baseball. It will be 108 years to date they have not had another World Series win. That's a long, long time Bubba. Yeah, I know but that doesn't really cut it to say that year was memorable for the ages. Well it is also the year that your favorite author of suspense and intrigue Daphne du Maurier was born. She inspired you to write your own story. Okay that's still not enough to make your claim. How about this. That year was also the time the Irish playwright John Millington Synge had his play "The Playboy of the Western World", debut at the Abbey Theater in Dublin, Ireland. Which causes several days of protest by theater goers? Okay, got it but why does that play memorable? Well it depicted a young man who is on the run from what he says he committed a crime against his father. He ran into a local tavern and told the patronages there that he indeed had killed his father with mighty stroke to the head Their reaction was one of amazement and he was thought of as sort of a hero for doing such a thing. The barmaid falls in love with him and the locals are more interested in vicariously enjoying his story than in condemning the immorality of his murderous deed. The play is best known for its use of the poetic, evocative language of Hiberno-English. It has several twists in the 2nd and 3 acts with the not so dead father returns to help save his son from the locals when they find out he did not kill his father which in turn made them so angry and thinking they were deceived made them want to kill him on the spot. Okay that sounds really something to read but it still isn't enough to make that year super *memorable. Oh yes it does my friend. Take this love affair that so many Trump Supporters have for a man who on countless times has said, "I could shoot someone and not loss one single vote". Also, his countless attacks on Women, People with disabilities, Gold Star Parents, and the list goes on and on. See the correlation there my friend. Yeah, wow you got me Bubba. Okay my friend let's see how the Trump Act 3 turns out. Yet to be determined.*

EPILOGUE IV

Bubba and I would like to give credit to the following who have inspired this Author to write this tale. 1. My wife who has stood by me for over 50 years through the good and bad times. Always a thoughtful mind with a very clear and pragmatic approach to all the issues problems facing our great country. 2. Our President, who show remarkable skills in communicating hope and restoring our economy from the pits of ruin and taking out so many terrorists without having a large body count of our men and women of the armed forces. He was able to lead us through the mire and chaos that was created not only from our enemies from afar but also his political adversary on the right side of the aisle. It was apparent right from the start of his term in office they would do anything to stop him from succeeding even if it put our Nation best interests in jeopardy. 3. The entire broadcasting crew at MSNBC. A breath of fresh air with tons of logic and good old common sense. Always fighting for the rights of us all. 3. Gabby Gifford heroic saga after her devastating wounding to start a crusade for reasonable gun control. It is a lesson to all that we can be knocked down, but we rise up again and look for justice and a safer world and that we as a country will not be intimidated by such wanton acts of violence and hate. 4 All the Gold Star Families who have given their love ones in the fight to protect our freedoms. We are all our in your debt. While living on Benedict Place, those many years ago during the World War II. One day a young man living two houses down came over to this young lad of 10 years of age. We had a delightful talk and he told me he was shipping out to go overseas and he couldn't tell where. He said would you like this air rifle? Wow yes, I would, and he gave it over to me with a broad smile. He said good bye and off he went. About a year later while riding my bike past his house I saw a small flag in the window. It had a gold star centered in the middle. Well later I asked my parents what did that mean? Sadly, they told me that was that young man had given his life to fight for our freedom and he was a credit to this great Nation. These heroic sacrifices are to be held close to our hearts for these deeds have are so instrumental in preserving our way of life and shall never be forgotten. This finishes up our Journey with the hopes of continue success against so many perils that we face as we go down our separate treks of life. So, to each of my readers have a super great trip of your own and pick up that pen and write your story today. Bubba and I wish you well and have one heck of a ride.

From Under The Palm Tree.

THE WINSOME SPRING

So that's how it happened. As your faithful Beagle, Hoppy nips at your heels, you both wander into yon field with smell's that kindle fond memories so potent you feel a tear drop falling listly aside. It's a game of marbles the line drawn in dirt. The sun shining on your head. The willow tree spread its branches high above. You feel once again the oneness but without any consciousness of thought. Mellow so true and strong, the moment it will never run its course. Time ever lasting for a lad to carry without any worry and with this in hand we know for sure Nothing better will happen this day. The smells so real with leash in hand you both stretch and lay the ground. Hoppy snort's his approval with a deep bellow of sorts and your hand stroke's his ears. What is better I say to remember such a day. Magical for you and without doubt everlasting to share without any qualms to fear. Another year comes our way.

A FAREWELL

From Under The Palm Tree Paulie The Ballie would like to share this his retirement from Saturday Shoot Out at the Link's course after 12 years at the helm. Doing what we like so much but it is time to say goodbye to that and move on to more writing of sorts with hope that we try with all our might to get it right. Here's a picture of the generous thoughtful trophy I got that final night. "Hey Bubba, can I say something"? "Sure Bubba, we have been doing this together for all those years". "I hear you are taking me on some kind of tour and that you are making me look like Charlie McCarthy. He is a dummy you know". "Okay, calm down you will be just fine and maybe bringing some chuckles to our friends in Assisted Living Facilities." "Say good bye now Bubba to all our readers". "So long and get going with your story it is more than worth it and have some fun in the sun." From Under The Palm Tree.

THE BRIAR PATCH

Here we are in the spirals of a Briar Patch
Mom told us never to enter such a place
But here's the catch
Try as we may there's no way to hack out
Each movement draw's some blood
And puts us further back
Well my friend what to do
One thing don't look to a hack
To settle all that.
We need to change how we back
Words alone will not be enough
We need true leadership
Showing to all our values
Will be restored and kept intact
With such a force making a tremendous impact
So, it looks like the Common Man must act.
And not to look to a distant hill for that.
From Under The Palm Tree

BREATH

O wondrous thing we took for granted for so long
During the youth of our life
Never took a brief moment to ponder
Too busy in that search
Running hither and yon
Always seeking and hoping for
Another day but Hey here's the rub
The search was in vain as you
Were there all along
Giving us so much and asking
Nothing in return
So, thanks for giving us this song
And each brand-new day
From Under The Palm Tree

THE WALMART GIRL

Year after year you were there for us
Always a smile and pleasantry
Keeping the sale simple without a fuss
Gracious with a kindred spirit of sort's
Looking for you every visit was a must
Time after time your service was with style
That made our shop worthwhile
Then one day you went away
Gone in a flash
No time to say Hey
Thank you for being so nice
We miss you hope you're okay
Just maybe we will meet up again one day
So, we can say, "Hey thanks and have a good life".
The message is loud and clear
For service such as that deserves a raise
Lift minimum wage to $15 an Hour
So, Congress don't be dowdy
And pass that raise without delay
So, all can say welcome to the 21st Century
From Under The Palm Tree

PROLOGUE & AN OPEN LETTER TO MY YOUNG READERS

Howdy young readers, Okay you are just beginning to see some things. You may be slightly unsure on what to think or what career to pursue or what to study. This is perfectly normal and not to worry. There is lots of time to decide and changing your first choice can be simply done after a good night's sleep. Here are some guide lines that I have found to be helpful: 1. Most important guard against the worst thing and that is Self-Doubt and do not let detractor's hold you back. Many will try to do this so simply reject that. 2. Keeping your health is also extremely important to make your journey last for at least 9 decades. I have found that my senior years are very rewarding and is like the whipped cream on a strawberry short cake. I for one found it to be the most creative time of my life. Being creative in whatever field one chooses is what gives us tremendous satisfaction and enhances one's self worth. I advise one to not smoke or drink alcohol. No need to inhibit your body with what have been known to affect the brain adversely killing brain cells. There is no need to use drugs. This life experience is enough of a stimulator and will take it from me be more than enough to keep one in awe. We live on a swirling planet that is held in space by gravity. Today we are on the door step of traveling to far distant planets and you will have a front row seat to that amazing stuff. The Tech. Is already in place and it is only a matter of time before man goes to Mars. I am currently working on a Science Fiction Novel about just that. A space ship manned by robot's that have been calibrated with minds of engineers, astrological scientist's, astronaut's and teacher's with PhD's in physics and mathematicians. They will all be answering to a master computer which I have named Mother T. Their space ship will be assembled on a space station and will be launched from there. Please stay tuned for that sometime early next year.

In conclusion not only will you have a front row seat to some very amazing advances in space travel but some of you may play an important role with the planning and execution of that. It is as my lead character Bubba always says, "A real gas of a ride".

LETTER TO TAMPA BAY TIMES

One more thing, Bubba says I should share my recent letter to the Tampa Bay Times so here it is.

A Salute To The All Pasco County Performing Band

Today 1/21/17, was an experience of why the arts are so important for our school age children. Both my Lovely and Moi went to see the All Pasco County Band perform at River Ridge School. Folks it was truly great performance. I have seen several Broadway Plays while living in New York and they couldn't hold a candle to these young boys and girls. These talented performers were magnificent and brought a tear to this old man's eye. Listening the Wizard of Oz melody was a trip back in time. All players where right on key. One left the building humming the tunes and feeling so blessed to have been able to watch this exceptional performance. The message is loud and clear leave the endowment for arts alone do not cut it. Our culture cries out for these young people to have a life in these arts if they so wish. It is truly a noble career and one that must be left open for these children. So, congress leave the Arts Budget alone. After leaving the building and walking to my car I saw many leaves on the ground and being in such good spirits I thought to write this poem.

"Leaves"

They fall like snowflakes curling to the ground

Gushes will propel them around and around

Their annual pilgrimage is so mindful of years gone pass

Jolts our memories with a dashing flash

Which gives this lad a pause for thought

A child in tow. Play's with abandonment

He rolls and turns in a pile of sorts

Back in time he dwells once more

A time so real it should be shared for all

For such a timeless moment will surely endure every fall

TWO CHICKS AT MY DOOR

Okay Bubba," This is an order do not open the front door until further notice." "Okay, how come?" "Well my friend we have four visitors making their home there with a nest of sorts in the wreath that is hanging on the overhead with two baby chicks just hatched and getting ready to venture into the world. It is remarkable how both papa and mama are tending to these newly hatched chicks. They are faithfully in attendance each day. Doting with pure dedication and caring." Bubba smiles and promises to not open the door. Truly a display of nature at work right before our very eyes.

If one gets really close a faint chirp, chirp is heard.
Each day it becomes louder and louder
Chirp on my fine feather visitor's
Grow up to fly away is our hope
And thanks for choosing our front door.
Have a good safe life and maybe you will
Be visiting our door once more.
There were two launching at different times
The larger chick only took 5 days to launch
The smaller one took 10 days after two aborts
But success on the third attempt
Hope to see you again some time
Have a great time out there you two
It has been a real gas to watch
Mother Nature at work right here at our front door

O WALT

O Walt, O Walt, What have we done?
Lost the way, I hear you say.
Tell us what to do this day.
Stay on track and not go back.
Stop hatred and fear my friend.
Just keep Liberty Bell chiming.
Let it ring loud and clear for all to hear.
And don't forget our Lady's Torch Giving
hope and solace is what we are about
Will we walk that path without losing the way?
It's so easy to do each day.
Sure, we will just like in year's gone past.
Some stumbles and lurches back
But with those lessons learned
We always get back on track
A diverse Nation still young
With a very good heart.
Showing compassion for the most part
And those doubter's will lose their fear
Thank you, Walt for all that.

DEFINE DESTINY

History tells us where to go or what path is the best without perils and pitfalls. Most will heed those lessons and proceed down their separate paths with discretion that results in successful achievements that give one tremendous satisfaction. A prime example is the hard-fought lessons learned from the great Civil War. Fighting for freedom for all peoples and that no man may own another was decided in a very decisive way. Today we have brought down many of those barriers that were held so furtively during those days before that tragic conflict. Integration of our Schools and Sports with all races have an opportunity to learn and compete without restrictions is what our Founding Fathers so eloquently stated in our Constitution. To see the mixing of all races in the fine state of fellowship is truly a blessing from God and brings a tear in this writer's eye. Now how does Define Destiny help along the way? Well now a good question so I to look back in time to show some compelling occurrences that really put this writer in awe. Was it by chance that I read an old letter my Father telling me about my Great Grandfather who fought in the Civil War as a young Union Soldier from Missouri? Or was its destiny to help me write about his wounding at Chancellorsville and his visit with the President Lincoln in Hospital. I think the latter is the answer. I am able to tell this to you by the grace of God as my Great Grandfather survived and prospered getting married and having four children which one was my Grandfather. The message from those begone days are loud and clear. Those hard fought for freedoms will not perish and will prevail so help us God. From Under The Palm Tree

THE CHILD OF MOSUL

In the pits of this Hell comes a wisp of humanity.

A young child alone devastated by forces beyond his control

An innocent victim is held tightly his head cradled by

A kindred fighter for justice and freedom

To be taken from this devastated land to a new home of sorts

Maybe to grow up strong and to help one day

To speak for a free country living in peace and hope
Be gone those merchants of death let your message
die completely from this Earth.
No purpose here so be gone, be gone never to return
With this in hand there is always hope and needs
just little push Inspiring others to this mission,
is our hope.

IN CLOSING

Every Society needs to have hope. Without it, life becomes a drudgery and causes countless problems for our way of life by affecting the National Mental Health and morale of all citizens. So, the need to recognize and give credit to those who have uplifted our spirits must be shared and given the due it so deserves. As a result, this poem ls dedicated to our retiring President Obama as he rides into the sunset with his family with his hat set ajar and his left arm hanging loosely from the saddle, we hear a distant voice saying, "Come back we all need you". Now the poem

Our Eight Year Legacy

His time in office, surely not to be forgotten will be etched in time
Steady was his hand that resounded throughout this land
With duly thoughtful act of mind of walking without fear
To keep us safe without body bags coming home to our shores
His eloquence rang true without any doubts and gave hope once more
For others to disregard and alter things will surely demean and set us back
Please, please keep us on this track and keep us moving forward and not back.
Let's keep those candles bright and stop the unprecedented attack on goodness and keep those beacons of light. Falsely cursing and claiming only darkness is such a waste and dangerous for us. March on good citizens,
March on with all you might even into the good night.

AFTER THOUGHT

Recently this writer was asked from a reader who had just read my new endeavor, "In the Light of Day". "Who is Bubba"? Bubba is my main character in both of my Endeavors. Including, Under The Palm Tree and he also makes an appearance in my new work titled "Y" a Play with 11 scene production soon to be published.

An interesting question. Just who is my lead character Bubba? After some serious thought here, it is.

Bubba represents the Common Man & Woman, the mail delivery person, the retail clerk, the factory worker, the law enforcement officers, first responders, nurses, teachers, Government workers who help keep us safe and protect our food and environment and air safety while travelling. All who are living from pay check to pay check. We see and deal with them daily and for the most part they are recognized as an important segment of our Society.

Bubba strives to see the good that is inherent in all well-meaning peoples. He is very much on his own and how he succeeds depends a lot on who represents us. He is ever Hopeful and tries his best to make the correct choices during his life's journey., There are however some destructive forces at work that need tending to and Bubba sees this and wants to do something about it. Too many are in harms' way. He wants to change some miss conceptions and better protect the public at large. His message is loud and clear to sound the alarm for a safer place for our children to grow up in,

Having hope for a better future is so important to maintain and must not be put asunder. That is his message.

"What do you think Bubba, did I get it right"? "Yup right on the money you old fart"."

Say goodbye, So long folks have a great journey and keep the faith. Amen

www.ingramcontent.com/pod-product-compliance
Lightning Source LLC
Chambersburg PA
CBHW031202020426
42333CB00013B/771